IS THE
END
NEAR?

STUDY GUIDE

**FRONT
LINE**

WHAT

JESUS

TOLD US

ABOUT THE

LAST DAYS

IS THE
END
NEAR?

STUDY GUIDE

MICHAEL YOUSSEF

Is THE END NEAR? STUDY GUIDE by Michael Youssef
Published by FrontLine, an imprint of Charisma Media
600 Rinehart Road, Lake Mary, Florida 32746

Visit the author's website at ltw.org, dryoussefbooks.com.

Cataloging-in-Publication Data is on file with the Library of
Congress.
International Standard Book Number: 978-1-63641-261-0
E-book ISBN: 978-1-63641-262-7

23 24 25 26 27 — 987654321
Printed in the United States of America

Most Charisma Media products are available at special
quantity discounts for bulk purchase for sales promotions,
premiums, fund-raising, and educational needs. For details,
call us at (407) 333-0600 or visit our website at www.
charismamedia.com.

A LETTER FROM
DR. MICHAEL YOUSSEF

D EAR FRIEND,
Welcome to the study guide for my book *Is the End
Near?*

As you will discover, this study guide is a wonderful companion to the book, as the study is designed to lead you deeper into God's Word. It is designed for a small group or even a large group study, but it will be quite useful for individual study as well.

Our study together will cover Matthew chapters 24 and 25, known as Jesus' Olivet discourse. As you may already know, the longest answer Jesus ever gave to a question was delivered on the Mount of Olives in response to His disciples asking, "What will be the sign of your coming and of the end of the age?" (Matt. 24:3).

This study guide is intended to be completed as a four-week Bible experience. Each week begins with a weekly session (a large study with sixty minutes of material for group or individual work) followed by five days of small studies, each set for fifteen minutes of individual work.

Over the next four weeks you will become well versed in Jesus' comprehensive teaching on the end times, and most importantly, you will learn how to be ready for His second coming.

Until the End,
Dr. Michael Youssef

FOUR-PART VIDEO SERIES

THE *Is the End Near? Study Guide* features exclusive access to a four-part video series with Dr. Michael Youssef, designed to enhance your study of Matthew 24 and 25.

Follow the prompts within this study guide and access the video series here:

LTW.org/ITENStudy

Password: **Matt24&25**

CONTENTS

Week 3: Watch for the End

Week 4: Faithful to the End

STUDY GUIDELINES

WELCOME TO THE *Is the End Near?* Bible study. During the course of the next four weeks, we will enjoy an in-depth exploration of Matthew chapters 24 and 25, the second-longest and most urgent teaching Jesus gave to His disciples. It is famously known as the Olivet discourse because He delivered the teaching on the Mount of Olives.

During our study together, we will learn of Jesus' promises and plans for what is known as *the end times*. It is fitting that we should closely examine the words of our Savior regarding His "going to prepare a place for us" (see John 14:3) and His imminent return. By studying Jesus' teaching to His followers, we will gain insight on how to live expectantly in a world unprepared for His second coming.

THE BOOK

The *Is the End Near? Study Guide* is a companion to my book *Is the End Near?: What Jesus Told Us About the Last Days*. As we progress through this study, each week will align with two chapters of the book. As such, we will often reference the book, and the book will contain the answers to many of the reflection questions.

Note: The study guide is designed to be used in concert with the book.

Study Format

The *Is the End Near? Study Guide* and video series are designed to be experienced either in a group setting (i.e., a small group gathering or a Sunday school class) or as individual study time. Each weekly session begins with a reflection question followed by watching the video message. (Streaming and DVD available.) Space is provided for you to take notes as you view the video.

After viewing the video, you will engage in a directed discussion, reflect on the memory verse, and close with a time of prayer. Feel free to adapt the format and flow of activities based on the size and structure of your group or to accommodate your personal study.

Four-Week Journey

A wonderful part of this guided study is the individual daily sessions designed to help you engage with the text more deeply. Each day you will read a passage of Scripture and then answer a set of reflection questions that will help you mine the material you surveyed during the weekly session. Additionally, there will be a review of the key verse as well as a time for prayer.

Each week consists of five daily sessions of verse-by-verse study. On the sixth day of each week you can reflect on the material learned that week (or catch up on any work you missed) in order to be ready for the next weekly session. As you work through the four-week study, you will read and reread and become very well versed in chapters 24 and 25 of Matthew.

GROUP STUDY

If you are doing the study with a group, each group member should have a copy of this study guide. Why? It will help everyone actively engage in the *weekly sessions*, as well as allow all group members to fully benefit from the enhanced enrichment of the *daily sessions*. Keep in mind the videos, questions, and activities are simply tools to help you engage with the session. The real transformation comes from digging into the Scriptures and manifesting the message.

Finally, each group needs a facilitator who is responsible for starting the video teaching and keeping track of time during discussions and activities. Facilitators may also prompt participants to contribute in the discussions to ensure that everyone has the opportunity to participate.

For more on the facilitator's role, please see the Facilitator's Guide included in the appendix of this study guide.

Introduction

THE GOSPEL OF MATTHEW

MATTHEW WAS ONE of the twelve disciples of Jesus. He is best known as the tax collector who was sitting at his tax booth when Jesus came by and said, "Follow Me." While the Gospel of Matthew is often attributed to the disciple Matthew, it was most likely assembled by an anonymous male Jew familiar with the technical aspects of Scripture.

AUDIENCE

The Gospel of Matthew is a work for second-generation Jewish Christians, for whom the defining event was the destruction of the temple by the Romans in AD 70. This audience is designated as Jewish Christians because they kept the Jewish customs while recognizing Jesus as Messiah. Thus, unlike the other Gospels, Matthew never bothers to explain the Jewish traditions.

DATE AND LOCATION

Most biblical scholars pinpoint the writing of Matthew's Gospel between AD 70 and 80. It is widely thought to be the second Gospel written, with Mark being the first. The author wrote for a community of Greek-speaking Jewish Christians most likely located in Antioch within Syria.

Content Structure

Unique to the Gospel of Matthew is its content structure. There are five blocks of narrative content that contain five major discourses. The intention is for the book to be read over the course of a week—one of the five narrative blocks each day, plus an introduction and a conclusion.

Book breakdown

- Chapters 1–2: Introduction (Genealogy and Nativity)

- Chapters 3–7: First Narrative/Discourse (Sermon on the Mount)

- Chapters 8–10: Second Narrative/Discourse (Miracles and Discipleship)

- Chapters 11–13: Third Narrative/Discourse (Kingdom of Heaven)

- Chapters 14–18: Fourth Narrative/Discourse (Claims and Conflict)

- Chapters 19–25: Fifth Narrative/Discourse (Temple and Olivet Discourse)

- Chapters 26–28: Conclusion (Passion and Great Commission)

MAJOR MESSAGE

The overarching intention of Matthew's Gospel is to present Jesus as King or Messiah and to persuade the Jewish community to accept and proclaim Him as such. Writing for a Jewish Christian audience, the author wanted to present Jesus as the Teacher who was even greater than Moses. This is the reason that Matthew quotes from the Old Testament more than any other Gospel writer does.

KEY VERSES

Jesus replied: "'Love the Lord your God with all your heart and with all your soul and with all your mind.' This is the first and greatest commandment. And the second is like it: 'Love your neighbor as yourself.' All the Law and the Prophets hang on these two commandments."

—MATTHEW 22:37–40

KEY THEMES

Several key themes emerge throughout the Book of Matthew:

- The Kingdom of Heaven (appears thirty-two times)—revealed the Jesus way

- The Law of Righteousness—affirmed the Mosaic law and Jewish tradition

- Fulfillment of Prophecies—enabled the Jews to recognize Jesus as Messiah

- The Second Coming—conveyed the message of what will happen in the end times before Jesus returns; *the focal point of our study*

WEEK 1
THE END IS COMING

Opening

THESE DAYS, PEOPLE both within and outside the church are increasingly asking the same question: "Is this the end of the world?" Christians phrase it differently, of course: "Are we in the end times?" But Christians and non-Christians alike are watching current events and coming to the same conclusion: history appears to be drawing to a close.

Prayer

Pray that we would be watching and waiting because *the end is coming.*

Question

> Do you think that we are living in the end times and Jesus is coming back soon? Why or why not?

Reading

Read Matthew 24:1–14. While reading this passage, write down any key insights or questions that come to your mind.

Watching

Watch the Week 1 video and take notes on your reflections and questions.

ACCESS THE VIDEOS HERE
LTW.org/ITENStudy
Or scan this QR code:

Password: **Matt24&25**

DISCUSSING

Questions

Use the following questions to help guide your discussion or reflection. Take time to consider some or all of the questions with your group members, or answer them in your individual study.

1. Dr. Michael Youssef believes we are witnessing events that the Bible foretold regarding the end times, events that Jesus foretold in Matthew 24 and 25. What do you think?

2. As believers, we can view the end of history not with alarm but with hope. However, most of us still have questions and concerns. What are some of yours?

3. There are many false gospels that circulated in biblical times and appear in our world today. Which of the following fake gospels are you most susceptible to?

- Prosperity gospel

- Progressive gospel

- Social gospel

- Libertarian gospel

- Other

4. Matthew 24:4–14 lists six "labor pains" that Christians will experience before the second coming of Christ:

- Falsehood and deception

- Wars and rumors of wars

- Famines and earthquakes

- Believers will be hated

- Apostasy

- Global evangelism

Which of these pains are you seeing today?
Which ones are you most concerned about?

5. Considering the chaos all around us and the coming doom that will happen before Jesus returns, how might we respond and even rejoice?

6. In light of Jesus' words of warning that we have learned together, are you ready for the second coming? What is the clearest sign that you are ready?

Closing

Encouragement

This coming week you will have the opportunity to go deeper into Matthew 24:1–14. The individual sessions that follow provide the path for you to Reflect, Read, Respond, and Rejoice at the words of Jesus as He shares of His second coming.

Prayer

- Lift up prayers of thanks and praise that Jesus came and will not leave us—He will rescue us when He comes again.

- Praise Jesus for not keeping us in the dark but rather sharing the signs and giving us the warning so we can be alert.

- Ask the Holy Spirit to grow your faith in Jesus. Pray that we as a group (or you individually) would live more urgently with the end in mind.

Weekly reading

Key scripture passage: Matthew 24:1–14

Book chapter 1: "Is This the End?"

Book chapter 2: "The Labor Pains of History"

Day 1

A WORD OF WARNING

REFLECT

IN JULY 2021, *The Nation* published a story titled "The End of the World Is Closer Than It Seems." In that piece, author Tom Engelhardt wrote that he worries the world will end in a nuclear holocaust. In 2020, even as a pandemic killed nearly two million people, nine nations were growing their nuclear arsenals. More than half of the expenditures for new nuclear weaponry—$37.4 billion—were laid out by the United States, including $13.3 billion for the development of intercontinental ballistic missiles. In total the nine nuclear-armed nations spent about $137,000 per minute to update a global nuclear arsenal that "could end history as we know it."[1]

READ

Matthew 23:1–4:

> Then Jesus said to the crowds and to his disciples: "The teachers of the law and the Pharisees sit in Moses' seat. So you must be careful to do everything they tell you. But do not do what they do, for they do not practice what they preach. They tie up heavy, cumbersome loads and put them on other people's shoulders, but they themselves are not willing to lift a finger to move them."

RESPOND

1. Jesus said there would be wars, rumors of wars, and economic crises in the end times as signs of divine judgment against disobedience. Do you believe we are living in the end times?

2. At the start of Matthew 23, what warning did Jesus give to the crowds and His disciples? What were the teachers of the law and the Pharisees doing?

3. In light of Jesus' words of warning, how might we give careful thought to our ways?

REJOICE

With today's learning in mind, give thanks to God in prayer.

THE CHARACTER OF CHRIST

REFLECT

JESUS' TEACHING ON the end times is not meant to frighten you but to serve as a warning. The reality is that you can be encouraged and hopeful. It is almighty God, not the atomic scientists, who holds the future in His hands. In His Word, God gave us a reliable and reassuring guide to the future. Jesus told us what to expect in the days before His return, and He assured us that we do not need to be anxious or afraid.

READ

Matthew 23:37–39:

> Jerusalem, Jerusalem, you who kill the prophets and stone those sent to you, how often I have longed to gather your children together, as a hen gathers her chicks under her wings, and you were not willing. Look, your house is left to you desolate. For I tell you, you will not see me again until you say, "Blessed is he who comes in the name of the Lord."

Respond

1. This scripture passage precedes Jesus' teaching on the end times. What do these verses show us about the character of our Savior?

2. Is your faith firmly anchored in the Lord Jesus Christ? If it is, then no dire circumstances or crises can shake your confidence. As a follower of Jesus, what can you be certain about?

3. Are you ready for the second coming of Jesus Christ? What is the clearest sign that you are ready?

Rejoice

With today's learning in mind, give thanks to God in prayer.

JESUS TAUGHT ABOUT THE END

REFLECT

EVER SINCE JESUS walked the dusty roads of Palestine, His followers have been asking, "Are we approaching the end times? When will the Lord Jesus return?" His disciples were as curious about the end times as we are today. And Jesus had much to say about the closing days of human history. In Matthew 24 we find the Lord's answer to His disciples' question, which He gave on Mount Olivet, or the Mount of Olives.

READ

Matthew 24:1–3:

> Jesus left the temple and was walking away when his disciples came up to him to call his attention to its buildings. "Do you see all these things?" he asked. "Truly I tell you, not one stone here will be left on another; every one will be thrown down." As Jesus was sitting on the Mount of Olives, the disciples came to him privately. "Tell us," they said, "when will this happen, and what will be the sign of your coming and of the end of the age?"

Respond

1. Why did the disciples call Jesus' attention to the temple buildings? What do you think they were wondering about?

2. Jesus' direct response about the temple—"Not one stone here will be left on another"—was a bold prediction. What was startling about it?

3. It was natural for the disciples to wonder when
   Jesus would end their oppression and restore
   the kingdom to Israel. Why were the disciples
   asking about the timing of events?

REJOICE

With today's learning in mind, give thanks to God in prayer.

THE BEGINNING OF PAINS

REFLECT

IN HIS ALERT to the end times, Jesus used the metaphor of labor pains to tell us the events associated with His second coming will intensify shortly before His return. In fact Jesus named six signs, or "labor pains," that foreshadow the conclusion of history. Each of these six signs has always been with us; the difference is that, like labor pains, they will become more frequent and more severe until Jesus appears.

READ

Matthew 24:4–8:

> Jesus answered: "Watch out that no one deceives you. For many will come in my name, claiming, 'I am the Messiah,' and will deceive many. You will hear of wars and rumors of wars, but see to it that you are not alarmed. Such things must happen, but the end is still to come. Nation will rise against nation, and kingdom against kingdom. There will be famines and earthquakes in various places. All these are the beginning of birth pains."

RESPOND

1. The first labor pains listed are falsehood and deception. Jesus warns His disciples (all of us), "Watch out that no one deceives you." Why are we prone to deception?

2. The second labor pains are wars and rumors of wars. The world today is a roiling cauldron of international tension. Why should we not be alarmed when we hear of conflicts and combats?

3. The third labor pain is famines and earthquakes. As terrifying as these can be, Jesus
   tells us this is just the beginning. How are we
   to respond to these natural disasters?

Rejoice

With today's learning in mind, give thanks to God in prayer.

MORE AND MORE PAINS

REFLECT

TODAY WE WILL continue to review the many signs Jesus gave regarding His second coming. In addition to deceptive people, raging conflicts, and natural disasters, Jesus spoke of persecution and renunciation as well as His message of grace spreading throughout the world. But as we have learned, we are not to be alarmed. We are to take heart, to be courageous and full of faith. Jesus said that such things must happen, "and then the end will come."

READ

Matthew 24:9–14:

> Then you will be handed over to be persecuted and put to death, and you will be hated by all nations because of me. At that time many will turn away from the faith and will betray and hate each other, and many false prophets will appear and deceive many people. Because of the increase of wickedness, the love of most will grow cold, but the one who stands firm to the end will be saved. And this gospel of the kingdom will be preached in the whole world as a testimony to all nations, and then the end will come.

Respond

1. The fourth labor pain is that believers will be hated by all nations. Why will we be hated as the end comes?

2. The fifth labor pain is apostasy. As persecution and pain intensify around the world, many believers will become apostates—they will forsake Christ and renounce their faith. Why will they defect?

3. The sixth and final labor pain is global evangelization, that the "gospel of the kingdom will be preached in the whole world." Are we getting close to reaching the globe for Christ?

REJOICE

With today's learning in mind, give thanks to God in prayer.

Day 6

REST AND REFLECT

TODAY, SPEND SOME time resting and reflecting on what you have learned this week, or catching up on any work you missed.

WEEK 2
SIGNS OF THE END

OPENING

JESUS TOLD US that before His return we would witness wars, famines, and catastrophes of all kinds. These crises are coming upon the world right now. They are already devastating the world economy and the lives of countless people. Jesus said one sign that He is coming soon is the sign of growing persecution: "Then you will be handed over to be persecuted and put to death, and you will be hated by all nations because of me" (Matt. 24:9). Every attack and insult you suffer for the Lord's sake is a signpost pointing to the imminent return of Jesus Christ.

Prayer

Pray that we would be watching and waiting for the *signs of the end.*

Question

> What are some signs in the atmosphere that signal a coming storm?

Reading

Read Matthew 24:15–35. While reading this passage, write down any key insights or questions that come to your mind.

Watching

Watch the Week 2 video and take notes on your reflections and questions.

ACCESS THE VIDEOS HERE
LTW.org/ITENStudy
Or scan this QR code:

Password: **Matt24&25**

DISCUSSING

Questions

Use the following questions to help guide your discussion or reflection. Take time to consider some or all of the questions with your group members, or answer them in your individual study.

1. There are many signs that the "end of the world as we know it" is coming soon. Is this a good thing? How are we to respond?

2. Bible-believing Christians have debated for centuries how and when the end will come and whether Christ-followers will be spared from the agony of the great tribulation. What do you think? Does it matter? Why or why not?

3. Interestingly, in today's passage, while talking of the "desolation to come" we see Jesus invoke the prophet Daniel. How does this affect your perspective on Daniel, and the Old Testament as a whole?

4. In Matthew 24:21 Jesus tells us "there will be great distress, unequaled from the beginning of the world until now—and never to be equaled again." Does this motivate you to do something? Warn others? Share the signs? Evangelize?

5. Many of Jesus' parables are agrarian in nature, including the parable of the fig tree (Matt. 24:32–35), because agriculture was the vocation of the day. What major point was Jesus making by using the fig tree? How might we communicate this point today?

6. Throughout the last two weeks we have learned a lot about what Jesus said regarding His return. Why do you think Jesus shared these signs of His second coming? How might His words prepare us for what is to come?

Closing

Encouragement

In this coming week you will have the opportunity to go deeper into Matthew 24:15–35. The individual sessions will provide the path for you to Reflect, Read, Respond, and Rejoice with the words of Jesus as He shares of His second coming.

Prayer

- Lift up prayers of thanks and praise that Jesus came and will not leave us—He will rescue us when He comes again.

- Praise Jesus for not keeping us in the dark but rather sharing the signs and giving us the warning to be alert.

- Ask the Holy Spirit to grow your faith in Jesus. Pray that we as a group (or you individually) would live more urgently with the end in mind.

Weekly reading

Key scripture passage: Matthew 24:15–35

Book chapter 3: "'Those Days' and 'That Day'"

Book chapter 4: "The Final Sign"

UNEQUALED DISTRESS

REFLECT

WE LIVE IN a world that is broken by sin. The only permanent peace this world will ever know is that future time when Jesus, the Prince of Peace, comes to rule for all eternity. But before the eternal reign of Jesus begins, the world must pass through a time of unprecedented terrors. Jesus tells us there will be great distress, unequaled from the beginning of the world until now. For unbelievers this will be a time of absolute despair, but for those who trust in Jesus these events will be a sign of hope, signaling that Jesus will soon come to take us to heaven.

READ

Matthew 24:15–21:

> So when you see standing in the holy place "the abomination that causes desolation," spoken of through the prophet Daniel—let the reader understand—then let those who are in Judea flee to the mountains. Let no one on the housetop go down to take anything out of the house. Let no one in the field go back to get their cloak. How dreadful it will be in those days for pregnant women and nursing mothers! Pray that your flight will not take place in winter or on the Sabbath. For then

there will be great distress, unequaled from the beginning of the world until now—and never to be equaled again.

Respond

1. In the passage today, Jesus mentions the prophet Daniel. Does this affirm the teachings of Daniel? Do you see it more as a "literal, physical prophecy" or a "figurative, spiritual prophecy"?

2. Jesus speaks of being on the housetop and being in the field before the flight from destruction. In the modern world, what places might be invoked today?

3. In the twenty-first century we talk about life being overwhelmingly stressful; however, *the great distress* will be unequaled. How does that make you feel?

REJOICE

With today's learning in mind, give thanks to God in prayer.

"THOSE DAYS"

REFLECT

IN TODAY'S PASSAGE Jesus continues to weave two separate events together. He speaks of what will happen in "those days" (*ekeinos hēmera*)—forty years after His ascension into heaven—as well as what will happen "at that time" (*tote*) when He comes again. In *those days*, the people of Israel had to flee to the mountains to escape the attack and destruction of the temple. *At that time*, false prophets and messiahs will arise to distort the Lord's message.

READ

Matthew 24:22–24:

> If those days had not been cut short, no one would survive, but for the sake of the elect those days will be shortened. At that time if anyone says to you, "Look, here is the Messiah!" or, "There he is!" do not believe it. For false messiahs and false prophets will appear and perform great signs and wonders to deceive, if possible, even the elect.

RESPOND

1. What did Jesus tell us would happen in "those days" (*ekeinos hēmera*, forty years after His ascension into heaven)? What were the expectations?

2. The "at that time" Jesus taught about is often referred to as the "great tribulation." Do you think we will be rescued before, during, or after the tribulation? (See 1 Thessalonians 4:16–17.)

3. Jesus warned us about *false messiahs and false prophets*. Who is sharing a false gospel message in our world today?

Rejoice

With today's learning in mind, give thanks to God in prayer.

Day 3

THE COMING SON OF MAN

REFLECT

IN MATTHEW 24:25 Jesus said, "See, I have told you ahead of time." In other words, He was giving a heads-up: "I have given you plenty of warning. Make sure you are prepared. Don't let that day take you by surprise. Make sure you and your family are ready for the end times." Jesus intimates that His return will not be stretched out over days or weeks—it will be sudden, glorious, and visible to the entire world.

READ

Matthew 24:25–28:

> See, I have told you ahead of time. So if anyone tells you, "There he is, out in the wilderness," do not go out; or, "Here he is, in the inner rooms," do not believe it. For as lightning that comes from the east is visible even in the west, so will be the coming of the Son of Man. Wherever there is a carcass, there the vultures will gather.

Respond

1. In Acts chapter 1, Jesus ascended into heaven, and the angels told the disciples that He would return in the same way. How does "lightning" fit with this characterization?

2. Jesus speaks of a carcass and vultures, which was a common idiom in Jewish culture. What does Jesus mean by invoking this expression? (See book pages 67–68.)

3. How should we respond to this message of warning and hope from Jesus, the Lord of history?

REJOICE

With today's learning in mind, give thanks to God in prayer.

HIS GLORIOUS APPEARING

REFLECT

THERE ARE INCREASING signs that Jesus' return may be growing near. As we see the persecution of Christians increasing worldwide—even in America—we must ask ourselves, Are we approaching the end times? Will the Lord Jesus return soon? Up to this point in the Olivet discourse Jesus has been telling the disciples about a time we call the great tribulation. Beginning with Matthew 24:29, He tells them what will happen *after* the great tribulation.

READ

Matthew 24:29–31:

> Immediately after the distress of those days "the sun will be darkened, and the moon will not give its light; the stars will fall from the sky, and the heavenly bodies will be shaken." Then will appear the sign of the Son of Man in heaven. And then all the peoples of the earth will mourn when they see the Son of Man coming on the clouds of heaven, with power and great glory. And he will send his angels with a loud trumpet call, and they will gather his elect from the four winds, from one end of the heavens to the other.

RESPOND

1. Jesus describes the immediate signs before the final sign—His glorious appearing. Are these immediate signs scientifically possible? Will "the world" be ready?

2. On the Mount of Transfiguration the disciples saw Jesus "shine like the sun." There are many other "light in the darkness" passages in Scripture. How is this consistent with Christ's return?

3. "On that day" the world will be shaken and
   panic will ensue. Where will the safe place be?
   Who will be in mourning?

REJOICE

With today's learning in mind, give thanks to God in prayer.

NEVER PASS AWAY

Reflect

THE PARABLE OF the fig tree is far less complicated than many people think. Jesus was simply giving the disciples a parable to make it easy for them—and us—to understand the signs of His return. Our Lord was saying, "When you see the fig leaves, you know the time of harvest is coming; when you see the signs, know that the day of judgment is coming soon." He was saying, "Wake up before it's too late." As He declared, these words of warning and promise have not passed away, and they never will.

Read

Matthew 24:32–35:

> Now learn this lesson from the fig tree: As soon as its twigs get tender and its leaves come out, you know that summer is near. Even so, when you see all these things, you know that it is near, right at the door. Truly I tell you, this generation will certainly not pass away until all these things have happened. Heaven and earth will pass away, but my words will never pass away.

RESPOND

1. Many of Jesus' parables were of an agrarian nature. Why might Jesus have chosen a fig tree for the parable about His coming? (See book page 82.)

2. The fig tree in spring represents a coming sign of harvest in the summer. What are some modern ways (other metaphors) we might express the second coming of Jesus?

3. Jesus stated that "this generation will certainly not pass away until all these things have happened." What generation was Jesus referring to? (See book pages 83–84.)

REJOICE

With today's learning in mind, give thanks to God in prayer.

REST AND REFLECT

TODAY, SPEND SOME time resting and reflecting on what you have learned this week, or catching up on any work you missed.

WEEK 3

WATCH FOR THE END

Opening

GOD DID NOT share biblical prophecy with us so we would know exactly what will happen and when it will take place. God gave us biblical prophecy to instruct us and encourage us to live holy lives. He wants us to live obediently and watch for His return, when the heavens will open and Jesus will appear. We don't know the day or the hour, but we know what God has called us to do: get ready!

Prayer

Pray that we would stay alert and be on guard, and *watch for the end.*

Question

What are some things you are always on the lookout for? Why?

READING

Read Matthew 24:36–51. While reading this passage, write down any key insights or questions that come to your mind.

WATCHING

Watch the Week 3 video and take notes on your reflections and questions.

ACCESS THE VIDEOS HERE
LTW.org/ITENStudy
Or scan this QR code:

Password: **Matt24&25**

DISCUSSING

Questions

Use the following questions to help guide your discussion. Take time to consider some or all of the questions with your group members, or answer them in your individual study.

1. After a couple weeks of learning, we are getting the message Jesus was giving: "Be on the lookout; watch for the signs of the end." Why do you think some Christians are not looking for the return of Christ?

2. In this week's passage Jesus mentions another Old Testament character: Noah. When Noah preached a message of repentance to his neighbors, they mocked and ridiculed him. How does this motivate you to share the good news with others?

3. Years ago there was a popular series of books called Left Behind. Was this a fictional account or a true version of what is going to happen? Will some people be left behind?

4. In Matthew 24:40–42 Jesus makes it clear that not all will be saved from the coming judgment. Are you going to be saved? Why will some not be saved?

5. In the illustration of the wise and the foolish servants we learn about the just reward of the faithful and the just result for the wicked. Is this a fair proposition for all people? Why or why not?

6. Regarding the end times coming, Jesus tells us to "Keep watch! Be on the lookout. Stand guard. Anticipate My return." How do we do this? What do you want to be doing when Jesus returns?

Closing

Encouragement

This coming week you will have the opportunity to go deeper into Matthew 24:36–51. The individual sessions will provide the path for you to Reflect, Read, Respond, and Rejoice with the words of Jesus as He shares of His second coming.

Prayer

- Lift up prayers of thanks and praise that Jesus came and will not leave us—He will rescue us when He comes again.

- Praise Jesus for not keeping us in the dark but rather sharing the signs and giving us the warning so we can be alert.

- Ask the Holy Spirit to grow your faith in Jesus. Pray that we, as a group (or you individually), would live more urgently with the end in mind.

Weekly reading

Key scripture passage: Matthew 24:36–51

Book chapter 5: "The Noah Imperative"

Book chapter 6: "Sudden—and Unexpected"

NO ONE KNOWS

REFLECT

JESUS SAID THAT no one but God knows the day when He will return. It could be today or a thousand years from now. Only the Father knows the precise timetable of the end times. Whenever the subject of the Lord's return is discussed, people seem to fall into two camps: (1) those who try to predict the date of His return and (2) those who are skeptical and apathetic about it. But Jesus tells us that His genuine followers will watch for His return.

READ

Matthew 24:36:

> But about that day or hour no one knows, not even the angels in heaven, nor the Son, but only the Father.

RESPOND

1. Why is it that some Christians are not expectantly looking for the return of Jesus?

2. Why have there been so many predictors of the time and place of Jesus' return?

3. Rather than predicting the time of Jesus'
   coming or not believing it will happen at all,
   what should we do?

REJOICE

With today's learning in mind, give thanks to God in prayer.

Day 2

AS IN THE DAYS OF NOAH

REFLECT

As we watch the news and see the wickedness all around us, we can't help but conclude that the days we live in have much in common with the days of Noah. We see widespread corruption and dishonesty in our government, greed and disloyalty in our corporations, and lust and blasphemy in our media. In this crucial section of the Olivet discourse the Lord Jesus compares the end times to the Noahic days found in the Book of Genesis. For those of us who heed the Scriptures there can be little doubt that the return of the Lord is imminent.

READ

Matthew 24:37–39:

> As it was in the days of Noah, so it will be at the coming of the Son of Man. For in the days before the flood, people were eating and drinking, marrying and giving in marriage, up to the day Noah entered the ark; and they knew nothing about what would happen until the flood came and took them all away. That is how it will be at the coming of the Son of Man.

RESPOND

1. Some people today believe the flood of Noah
   is a fable, not a real historical event. Why
   should we believe it really happened? (See book
   page 96.)

2. The same godless attitudes, desires, hatred, lust,
   and moral depravity that characterized Noah's
   time will prevail in the end times. Are we
   there yet?

3. For the unbeliever, the one who is not looking for the Lord's return, how will it be at the coming of the Son of Man?

REJOICE

With today's learning in mind, give thanks to God in prayer.

KEEP WATCH

Reflect

AT SOME FUTURE date known only to the Father, Jesus will return suddenly. Only those who are anticipating His return will rejoice on that day; everyone else will despair. It will all happen very quickly. People will be working side by side; one will be taken to heaven, and the other will be left behind to face the judgment. Be ready. Keep watch.

Read

Matthew 24:40–44:

> Two men will be in the field; one will be taken and the other left. Two women will be grinding with a hand mill; one will be taken and the other left. Therefore keep watch, because you do not know on what day your Lord will come. But understand this: If the owner of the house had known at what time of night the thief was coming, he would have kept watch and would not have let his house be broken into. So you also must be ready, because the Son of Man will come at an hour when you do not expect him.

RESPOND

1. Jesus made it abundantly clear that on the day of judgment, not everyone will be saved. This parable says "one will be taken and the other left." Will it be 50/50?

2. We can know the signs of the times, the signs that point to the Lord's imminent return, but *no one knows* the day or the hour when He will return. What frustrates you about knowing, but not knowing?

3. Why would Christians full of Christlike compassion withhold the good news from the people around them who might get left behind?

REJOICE

With today's learning in mind, give thanks to God in prayer.

THE FAITHFUL SERVANT

REFLECT

JESUS SHARED AN illustration of a wise and faithful servant, whom He subsequently contrasted with a foolish and wicked servant. Jesus made it clear that on the day of His return there will be a separation between believers and nonbelievers, between those who love the Lord and those who are not genuine Christians. Today we will learn about the reward for the faithful servant.

READ

Matthew 24:45–47:

> Who then is the faithful and wise servant, whom the master has put in charge of the servants in his household to give them their food at the proper time? It will be good for that servant whose master finds him doing so when he returns. Truly I tell you, he will put him in charge of all his possessions.

RESPOND

1. Jesus said there will be a separation between the believers and the nonbelievers. Are Christians really that different from non-Christians?

2. In Matthew 7:13 Jesus sounded an unambiguous warning: "Enter through the narrow gate." What is the narrow gate, and how do we go through it?

3. According to this parable, what is the reward for the faithful servant, the follower of God?

Rejoice

With today's learning in mind, give thanks to God in prayer.

Day 5

THE WICKED SERVANT

Reflect

WE FREQUENTLY HEAR people substitute their own wishful thinking in place of the clear warnings of Jesus. They say, "I just can't believe that a God of love would send anyone to hell." The reality, of course, is that people choose hell by disobeying God's truth. No one in the Bible spoke more about hell than Jesus Himself. He spoke more about hell than He spoke about heaven, and He described hell in the most dire and vivid terms.

Read

Matthew 24:48–51:

> But suppose that servant is wicked and says to himself, "My master is staying away a long time," and he then begins to beat his fellow servants and to eat and drink with drunkards. The master of that servant will come on a day when he does not expect him and at an hour he is not aware of. He will cut him to pieces and assign him a place with the hypocrites, where there will be weeping and gnashing of teeth.

Respond

1. What does this parable reveal about the character of a wicked servant?

2. Jesus uses the most dire and vivid terms to describe hell—weeping and gnashing of teeth. Do you think this is literal or figurative language?

3. One of the toughest questions people have is, "Why would a loving God send people to hell?" What is your answer to this question?

REJOICE

With today's learning in mind, give thanks to God in prayer.

REST AND REFLECT

Today, spend some time resting and reflecting on what you have learned this week, or catching up on any work you missed.

WEEK 4

FAITHFUL TO THE END

OPENING

THE RETURN OF Jesus Christ will be sudden and tragic for those who are unprepared—but that day will not take faithful believers by surprise. Those who are watching and waiting for the day of the Lord, those who are prepared to meet Him at any time, will rejoice in that moment. The faithful will arise to be with Christ in glory forever.

Prayer

Pray that we would get ready, boldly endure, and be *faithful to the end.*

Question

> Who are some of the people in your life who you can count on? Why?

Reading

Read Matthew 25:1–46. While reading this passage, write down any key insights or questions that come to your mind.

Watching

Watch the Week 4 video and take notes on your reflections and questions.

ACCESS THE VIDEOS HERE
LTW.org/ITENStudy
Or scan this QR code:

Password: **Matt24&25**

Discussing

Questions

Use the following questions to help guide your discussion. Take time to consider some or all of the questions with your group members, or answer them in your individual study.

1. The end times are coming, if they're not already here, and we are called to be faithful in the midst of the chaos. What does being faithful look like in your life? In the church as a whole?

2. In chapter 25 of Matthew, Jesus shared three parables illustrating what the end is going to yield for all of us. Why do you think Jesus chose to share this knowledge in parables? Are the stories meant to warn or encourage us?

3. Is there one of the following parables that resonates with you with more than the others? Is there one or more that you find confusing or concerning?

- The parable of the ten virgins

- The parable of the bags of gold (talents)

- The parable of the sheep and the goats

4. Each of these separation parables urges us to examine our lives and be ready for what is coming. What does it look like to be found wise versus foolish? Are you prepared to pass the test?

5. Since there is going to be "weeping and gnashing of teeth" for those who do not trust in Christ and are not looking for His second coming, what are you doing to make a difference? What can we do together?

6. There is only one question left to answer, and it is one that we have considered over and over again: If Jesus were to return today, are you ready to meet Him face to face?

Closing

Encouragement

This coming week you will have the opportunity to go deeper into Matthew 25:1–46. The individual sessions will provide the path for you to Reflect, Read, Respond, and Rejoice with the words of Jesus as He shares of His second coming.

Prayer

- Lift up prayers of thanks and praise that Jesus came and will not leave us—He will rescue us when He comes again.

- Praise Jesus for not keeping us in the dark but rather sharing the signs and giving us the warning so we can be alert.

- Ask the Holy Spirit to grow your faith in Jesus. Pray that we as a group (or you individually) would live more urgently with the end in mind.

Weekly reading

Key scripture passage: Matthew 25:1–46

Book chapter 7: "The Great Separation"

Book chapter 8: "True Security in a Collapsing World"

BE PREPARED

Reflect

WE COME NOW to the last week of our study and the second half of the longest answer Jesus ever gave to a question. The sheer length and depth of Jesus' reply to His disciples (Matt. 24–25) speaks volumes about the importance He places on the second coming. Today, through the parable of the ten virgins, Jesus encourages us to live with expectation and be prepared for His return.

Read

Matthew 25:1–13:

> At that time the kingdom of heaven will be like ten virgins who took their lamps and went out to meet the bridegroom. Five of them were foolish and five were wise. The foolish ones took their lamps but did not take any oil with them. The wise ones, however, took oil in jars along with their lamps. The bridegroom was a long time in coming, and they all became drowsy and fell asleep.
>
> At midnight the cry rang out: "Here's the bridegroom! Come out to meet him!" Then all the virgins woke up and trimmed their lamps. The

foolish ones said to the wise, "Give us some of your oil; our lamps are going out."

"No," they replied, "there may not be enough for both us and you. Instead, go to those who sell oil and buy some for yourselves."

But while they were on their way to buy the oil, the bridegroom arrived. The virgins who were ready went in with him to the wedding banquet. And the door was shut. Later the others also came. "Lord, Lord," they said, "open the door for us!"

But he replied, "Truly I tell you, I don't know you."

Therefore keep watch, because you do not know the day or the hour.

Respond

1. The parable of the ten virgins is the story of a test. Is it fair for God to test His people?

2. The five foolish virgins represent people who are "inside the church" but are not prepared. What are the profiles of these foolish virgins?

3. This parable ends with the same command we have already heard: "Keep watch." Will you heed this command? Are you ready to pass the test?

REJOICE

With today's learning in mind, give thanks to God in prayer.

BE GOOD AND FAITHFUL

REFLECT

ON THE HEELS of the parable of the ten virgins Jesus told another story—the parable of the bags of gold. It is a lesson about three servants who were given different amounts of money to manage. Through this parable Jesus implores us to take responsibility and do our duty, which will lead to sharing in His happiness.

READ

Matthew 25:14–23:

> Again, it will be like a man going on a journey, who called his servants and entrusted his wealth to them. To one he gave five bags of gold, to another two bags, and to another one bag, each according to his ability. Then he went on his journey. The man who had received five bags of gold went at once and put his money to work and gained five bags more. So also, the one with two bags of gold gained two more. But the man who had received one bag went off, dug a hole in the ground and hid his master's money.
>
> After a long time the master of those servants returned and settled accounts with them. The man who had received five bags of gold brought

the other five. "Master," he said, "you entrusted me with five bags of gold. See, I have gained five more."

His master replied, "Well done, good and faithful servant! You have been faithful with a few things; I will put you in charge of many things. Come and share your master's happiness!"

The man with two bags of gold also came. "Master," he said, "you entrusted me with two bags of gold; see, I have gained two more."

His master replied, "Well done, good and faithful servant! You have been faithful with a few things; I will put you in charge of many things. Come and share your master's happiness!"

RESPOND

1. This parable is often referred to as "the parable of the talents." Why does our Bible translation use "bags of gold"? (See book pages 142–143.)

2. Each servant was given a different number of gold bags. Is this fair?

3. Even though they were given different amounts, the first two servants received the same kudos and reward. Is this fair?

4. In your life, do you feel as though you have been given five bags, two bags, or one bag of gold? Are you pleased with your allotment?

REJOICE

With today's learning in mind, give thanks to God in prayer.

DON'T BE WICKED AND LAZY

REFLECT

IN THE PARABLE of the bags of gold, the gold bags represent the good news Jesus has imparted to us. What will we say to Jesus when He asks for an account of the way we used our lives? Will we present to Him people we have witnessed to over our lifetime? Or will we say, "I was afraid, so I didn't witness to anyone and kept Your good news hidden"?

READ

Matthew 25:24–30:

> Then the man who had received one bag of gold came. "Master," he said, "I knew that you are a hard man, harvesting where you have not sown and gathering where you have not scattered seed. So I was afraid and went out and hid your gold in the ground. See, here is what belongs to you."
>
> His master replied, "You wicked, lazy servant! So you knew that I harvest where I have not sown and gather where I have not scattered seed? Well then, you should have put my money on deposit with the bankers, so that when I returned I would have received it back with interest. So take the bag of gold from him and give it to the one who has ten bags. For whoever has will be given more,

and they will have an abundance. Whoever does not have, even what they have will be taken from them. And throw that worthless servant outside, into the darkness, where there will be weeping and gnashing of teeth."

Respond

1. In the parable, what drives the man who was given one bag of gold to hide it? How does he characterize the master?

2. The master orders the "worthless servant" to be thrown outside, "where there will be weeping and gnashing of teeth." Was the master unfair? Why or why not?

3. Before Jesus left this earth, He gave us a task,
   which we call the Great Commission. How are
   you investing in the sharing of the gospel?

Rejoice

With today's learning in mind, give thanks to God in prayer.

Day 4

YOU WHO WILL BE BLESSED

REFLECT

TODAY AND TOMORROW we finish Matthew 25—and our study—with a third parable: the parable of the sheep and the goats. This is another story illustrating the great separation at the end of time. For those who are found in Christ, blessing is sure to come.

READ

Matthew 25:31–40:

> When the Son of Man comes in his glory, and all the angels with him, he will sit on his glorious throne. All the nations will be gathered before him, and he will separate the people one from another as a shepherd separates the sheep from the goats. He will put the sheep on his right and the goats on his left.
>
> Then the King will say to those on his right, "Come, you who are blessed by my Father; take your inheritance, the kingdom prepared for you since the creation of the world. For I was hungry and you gave me something to eat, I was thirsty and you gave me something to drink, I was a stranger and you invited me in, I needed clothes and you clothed me, I was sick and you looked

after me, I was in prison and you came to visit me."

Then the righteous will answer him, "Lord, when did we see you hungry and feed you, or thirsty and give you something to drink? When did we see you a stranger and invite you in, or needing clothes and clothe you? When did we see you sick or in prison and go to visit you?"

The King will reply, "Truly I tell you, whatever you did for one of the least of these brothers and sisters of mine, you did for me."

RESPOND

1. Why might Jesus have chosen sheep and goats as the subjects of this parable? What are the differences between sheep and goats? (See book page 147.)

2. The King praises the faithful sheep for specific actions: giving food and water, providing hospitality, supplying clothing, and so on. What are other ways we can serve Jesus, our King?

3. Jesus said, "My sheep listen to my voice; I know them, and they follow me" (John 10:27). How can you follow Him more closely in your life?

REJOICE

With today's learning in mind, give thanks to God in prayer.

YOU WHO WILL BE CURSED

REFLECT

IN THE PARABLE of the sheep and the goats, the goats may have been very religious people who did good deeds, but these are not the same as having a relationship with the Good Shepherd. Those who think their religion or good deeds qualifies them as "sheep" will be devastated to discover they were really "goats" after all.

READ

Matthew 25:41–46:

> Then he will say to those on his left, "Depart from me, you who are cursed, into the eternal fire prepared for the devil and his angels. For I was hungry and you gave me nothing to eat, I was thirsty and you gave me nothing to drink, I was a stranger and you did not invite me in, I needed clothes and you did not clothe me, I was sick and in prison and you did not look after me."
>
> They also will answer, "Lord, when did we see you hungry or thirsty or a stranger or needing clothes or sick or in prison, and did not help you?"
>
> He will reply, "Truly I tell you, whatever you did not do for one of the least of these, you did not do for me."

Then they will go away to eternal punishment,
but the righteous to eternal life.

Respond

1. Jesus mentioned putting the sheep on the right
   and the goats on the left. What should we *not*
   read into this separation?

2. One might ask, "With Jesus speaking of good
   deeds, isn't He saying that good works are
   a qualification for salvation?" What is your
   response?

3. In earthly nature, a sheep can never become a goat; however, a nonbeliever can become a believer in Christ. Who can you tell about the Great Shepherd today?

REJOICE

With today's learning in mind, give thanks to God in prayer.

Day 6

REST AND REFLECT

TODAY, SPEND SOME time resting and reflecting on what you have learned this week, or catching up on any work you missed.

Conclusion

CLOSING PRAYER

Dear God,

While false believers all over the world spread fake gospels and defect from the truth, I thank You that Your true believers are joyfully paying the cost of following Jesus. We are grateful that Your people are spreading the good news of Jesus Christ to the far corners of the globe.

In our generation, may Your Great Commission of Your gospel of grace and Your kingdom of justice carry forward. May we do our part in the spreading of this message so that all nations might be reached— and then, as Jesus said, the end will come!

Come, Lord Jesus.

Amen.

FACILITATOR'S GUIDE

BEING A FACILITATOR of a study group is an important responsibility. As you may know, facilitating a group can make a big difference in the lives of others and can have a major influence for generations. It will also greatly impact your own walk with Jesus. So, thank you for choosing to make this happen.

As you will see, the *Is the End Near?* study is built around video content and small-group interaction.

As the group facilitator, you can be considered the master of ceremonies. You are the one who will plan and prepare for the group's enlightenment and enjoyment. As the facilitator, you do not need to teach the content or have all the answers; your role is simply to facilitate the experience for the group.

Before the first meeting, make sure everyone in the group has a copy of the book *Is the End Near?* as well as this study guide. This will ensure that all participants get the most from the weekly (group) and daily (individual) studies. It will keep everyone on the same page and help the learning run smoothly. Please tell your group members they are free to write in their study guides and should bring them to the group study each week.

SETUP

Your group will need to determine how long you want to meet each week so you can plan your time accordingly.

Generally most groups like to have the study for sixty or ninety minutes. The following is a suggested schedule:

Section	60-Minute Study	90-Minute Study
Opening (pray and discuss the opening question)	10 minutes	10 minutes
Reading (read the passage and reflect on key insights)	5 minutes	5 minutes
Watching (watch the video together and take notes)	15 minutes	15 minutes
Discussing (discuss the questions based on the video teaching)	25 minutes	45 minutes
Closing (reflect on key insights and pray together)	5 minutes	15 minutes

As the group leader, you want to create an environment that encourages learning and sharing. It is best to choose a casual environment with comfortable seating, like a family room or living room. This way, group members will be more relaxed and open. Additionally, you want to choose a setup that works for watching the video as well as sharing together. A smiling face, a warm welcome, and simple refreshments will go far in creating the best atmosphere for group study.

Note: Based on your group members' stages of life, you may want to consider offering childcare for couples with children.

Opening

Open the meeting with a short prayer based on the focus for the week. Next, give several people an opportunity to answer the opening question.

Reading

Invite a group member or two to read the passage for the session. After the reading, ask participants to share any insights that came to mind. It will be beneficial to hear from several members of the group.

Watching

Push play and watch the video teaching together. Encourage all group members to take notes and generate questions for the discussion time.

Note: Before you convene the group, be sure the media technology is working properly.

Discussing

After Reading and Watching, you and your group members are ready for Discussing. Encourage each member to participate in the discussion, but make sure they know it is not mandatory. (You don't want anyone to feel pressured.) As the discussion progresses, follow up with comments such as "Tell me more about that" or "Why did you answer that way?" This will allow for deeper reflection and invite meaningful conversations.

Note: The study guide includes multiple questions to use for the discussion, and you do not need to use them all. Feel free to pick and choose or to reorder the questions based on how the conversation goes. As the facilitator, you should make sure that no one person dominates the discussion and each person gets an opportunity to share.

Closing

Close by taking a few minutes for final reflections and prayer. Thank everyone for coming and being a part of the group.

NOTE

1. Tom Engelhardt, "The End of the World Is Closer Than It Seems," *The Nation*, July 2, 2021, https://www.thenation.com/article/world/nuclear-apocolypse/.

Connect with
Dr. Michael Youssef!

Follow Dr. Youssef for life-giving truth, behind-the-scenes ministry updates, and much more.

MichaelYoussef.com

 MichaelAYoussef

 Michael A. Youssef

Biblical Encouragement for You—Anytime, Anywhere

Leading The Way with Dr. Michael Youssef is passionately proclaiming uncompromising Truth through every major form of media, empowering you to know and follow Christ. There are many FREE ways you can connect with Dr. Youssef's teachings:

- Thousands of sermons and articles online
- TV and radio programs worldwide
- Apps for your phone or tablet
- A monthly magazine, and more!

Learn more at **LTW.org/Connect**